RADIO DAYS

라디오 데이즈

Radio Days

by Ha Jaeyoun

Translated by Sue Hyon Bae

Black Ocean
Boston · Chicago

라디오 데이즈

Originaly published in Korea by Moonji Publishing Co., Ltd in 2006
English edition is published by arrangement with
Moonji Publishing Co., Ltd

Black Ocean
P.O. Box 52030
Boston, MA 02205
blackocean.org

Cover Art and Design by Abby Haddican | abbyhaddican.com
Book Design by Taylor D. Waring | taylordwaring.com

ISBN: 9781939568724
Library of Congress Control Number: 2023938187

This book was published with the support of a publication and translation grant from the Literature Translation Institute of Korea (LTI Korea).

FIRST EDITION

Printed in Canada

CONTENTS

PART 3

PART 4

You say goodbye,
I say hello.
It reminds me of The Beatles.
How long have I known this music?

Early winter, 2006
Ha Jaeyoun

TRANSLATOR'S INTRODUCTION

I knew right away, when I discovered Ha Jaeyoun, that I wanted to translate her work, and that it would be fun labor. Though translation always has its challenges due to being basically impossible, translating *Radio Days* went well with my style of faithfulness. My previous translation work was on Kim Hyesoon, who challenges the readers with bold, violent imagery and poems difficult to pin down. In comparison, Ha Jaeyoun's poetry is vibrantly alive, and the most important goal was conveying her tone and language. Many long phrases and prepositions had to be excised during editing.

My translation approach is fairly rigid in that I have strong ideas about faithfulness. I try to avoid making the translation easier than the original poem and to keep original ambiguities, even when it takes more effort than producing a smoother experience for the reader.

I really enjoyed reading this book, including all the unanswered questions, so I want you to have as much of the same experience as I did. At the same time, Ha always has a light touch, so the language has to stay unpretentious and clear. I regret that I couldn't convey perfectly Ha's humor, wordplay, and unsaid gaps.

One problem that cropped up many times was that in Korean, pronouns are not as obligatory as in English, and third-person pronouns are in any case often gender-neutral. Thus, many Korean poems have a certain neutrality that is not possible with grammatically correct English, such as not knowing if the speaker is an "I" or "you," or if the person being addressed is a "he" or "she." I was extremely pleased about being able to keep the child genderless in "Corridor's Child" but had to make decisions for the reader in several others. For example, the other person in "Foam" is unspecified in the original, and initially in translation was "he" and later "she."

A similar ambiguity exists with the Korean 안녕 annyŏng, which can mean "hello" or "goodbye" depending on context. Any time you see a "hello" or "goodbye" in this book, that reflects my decision. In "Above the Highway," for example, I translated the first line with annyŏng as "We don't say hello" and the second line as "We don't say goodbye," probably because The Beatles reference at the start of *Radio Days* put into mind the song "Hello, Goodbye."

Finally, there is punctuation, my own personal translation obsession. I try to change punctuation as little as possible, taking into account differences in punctuation rules and customs. You may see a poem with inconsistent punctuation and wonder why that is. I, too, wonder, but I don't want to change it—I want you to wonder with me. I do make concessions, such as putting in commas in prose poems that originally had no punctuation at all, because while Korean is still fairly easy to understand without punctuation, English prose really isn't. But I kept in other elements that I think are important visual effects, such as the mystery comma at the very end of "My Own Life." Why does the poem end with a comma? I don't know and can't presume to answer for anybody else.

But all of this is making it sound as though *Radio Days* were an obscure and obtuse book. It is, in fact, a wonderfully pleasant and whimsical experience, and I hope you can feel, as I did, the humidity and wonder of Korean summers spent watching Paul's Miraculous Adventure and counting the Sundays.

"I Dream of School" and "Stella Beauty Parlor" were previously published in Action Books Blog, August 2021; "Chair" and "Cloud's Table" were published in volume 25 of *Water~Stone Review*, 2022. I would also like to thank the Literature Translation Institute of Korea for the translation grant for *Radio Days*, Jake Levine for the huge amount of editing work, and, of course, Ha Jaeyoun, who provided crucial feedback and encouragement.

Part 1
We, Like Fish

WHISTLING

Shadows tinged many colors
A bicycle's silver wheels roll away into the dark

A mother hollers her child's name
Next to the bench someone's left behind
a small doll

Fluttering up the clock tower, a dove,
the air
briefly wavers

Bench, park, night, nothing matters

STAIRCASE IN HEAVEN

Your footsteps are noiseless
A cat's soul
Children don't fear you
Time's lingered on you for ages
If you took some from me
I could be with you forever
I want to hold on gently to the wrinkle of you
If my body's red blood coagulated cell by cell
it would make a map as fresh as a leaf's xylem
It's fine if you just look
One two three I'll fall asleep
And there you are like you're trying to run

SIMULTANEOUSLY

In that moment she turned the page and
the man in the car with the doors open ran it off the cliff and
the cat nudged the coffee cup on the table and
the carpet fluttered a little and
the clock's broken second hand revolved twelve times and
the boy cut the marathon finish line tape and
she prayed for good luck but
both hands grew wrinkled and
hair grew thin and
the coffee spilled and the carpet didn't get wet and
the man flew under the green roof

BUTTERFLY EFFECT

Last night watching the pigs that had gotten on the rooftop
You get drunk and into fisticuffs with the taxi driver
The rain pours madly on screen

The house has no owners, its roof is gray or blue
The pigs don't care which roof
The mud runs red

A tiger swallowtail butterfly flaps smiling
Its pattern can frighten enemies
Its smile can pierce it on a pin

I have to watch its back carefully to keep pace
As soon as I go near
the expression on its back collapses

I always get overtaken on the road
because anything that gets passed is always left behind

Never mind the pigs' summer
Never mind the swallowtails' summer

A bird flies quietly
between apartment buildings 103 and 105
The bird doesn't leave an arc in the sky

THE SUNDAYS OF AUGUST

The good thing about dealing with me is I have each and every size, if you want the Sunday me I can put on a butterfly suit, one that seems about to fly away, if you want the dizziness of pattern on pattern, that eye, if it's that black helix pattern with no end in sight

The small cabbage white butterfly sits on cabbage and the tiger swallowtail butterfly has nowhere to go, in August there are four Sundays, one Sunday passes, I hang radish sprouts in the veranda, the second Sunday comes, the radish sprouts grow roots, four Sundays in August

Some Sunday, the bloodless revolution of a man wearing a ski mask on TV, the chair in front of the window, a long empty chair, the Sunday me doesn't sit in empty chairs, the good thing about dealing with me is I have each and every size, other Sundays I sit in the long chair, leaving sunlight and stains on the window

SUNDAY'S ANTIQUE SHOP

Into Sunday's antique shop
indirect sunlight leaks in
I'm the person passing by

In Sunday's antique shop
the Pierrot of loneliness prays
and I'm the person looking in

Stepping on broken pavement
counting fish swimming in the road
One or two cars passing by

Alleys open into alleys
but some alleys are blind
Closed shops in Sunday's alley

Maybe something's open there
but now I'm the person who can't remember
where indirect sunlight leaks

FOAM

She might have been a real person, but why did what I said to her echo back with a clang? About foam, the only thing I can say is the dizzying beauty of soap bubbles in my childhood

I become many circles and fly to the other side, the me on this side can't see how far the circles reach, my round mouth keeps making more of me, red orange green

On this side I'm still me, on the other side she is a never-ending picture, her face brightens and fogs and the clouds bite each others' tails while her expression makes raindrops elsewhere

Over my pupils now transparent I look at her, maybe I'm looking at her from a little while ago, a little while later she still hasn't disappeared, in that case have I been looking at the real her?

LIKE A ROSE VINE

My hair grows towards the window
Like a fool I close my eyes

I want to crunch and eat the glass cup
On weekends I'm thirsty

If I get some sleep and wake up
I think I can start from the beginning

Where do beautiful thorns
sprout for the first time?

While the pill bottles quietly stay awake all night
blood vessels spread below my wrists

My skin gets thinner
I think my eyelashes are growing longer

MERCHANT OF FOUR SEASONS

Drug store
The pill bottles are colorful and the magazines are packaged demurely, somebody opens the door, *bang*, the round mirrors surveil the cowboy hat, the music is bebop, tranquilizers like red green yellow flowerbeds, the cowboy holding a single flower slips away into the sound of rain

Merchant of Four Seasons
Nothing's gonna change my world, people drifting as slowly as a cloud changing shape, in this street I'm discovered by everybody and I'm pleasant air, if you fill up a bag with lustrous paprika red green yellow they'll go back to set the dinner table, nothing's gonna change my world

2-Person Devoré Sofa
14-inch TV, portable CD player, flight to Denmark, pine trees snowed on, chicken rice bowl, lunchbox, sturdy mug, the rain sounds of, the high windows and plaza, 2-person, white devoré sofa, alarm clock, cosmos of glow-in-the-dark minute and hour hands, the numbers can't be seen in the dark, the short needle and long needle move quietly and cross the universe, from the opposite side I can hear the fluttering sound of falling feathers

Round Library
In the library where the air circles all the way from the ceiling to the
first floor, the child is reading with wriggling toes, fingerprints a child
left a hundred years ago linger on the pages but nobody pays any mind,
the library ceiling is open to the sky, the librarian stamps barcodes until
nobody is born, and the child has twitchy feet until nobody is born,
bang, traces of someone who's gone

PERFUME

One footstep doesn't erase another. Who spilled the bad smell in the garden?

Like a butterfly's scent gnawing at a pansy, like two eyes that shine only at night left behind in the swallowtail butterfly's heart

a dirty shadow makes a cloud and the cloud calls and gathers more clouds. So who got lost in the garden? Like the footsteps of a herd of wet sheep

a fishy smell, birds drop black feathers. A tomb of feathers, and they are born above that tomb but,

nobody can smell their own smell, not here

FOR FIVE MINUTES

The difficult thing is a question of determination, that cloud must've decided to linger for five minutes, after five minutes the cloud might shift endlessly, the important thing is the five minutes I'm watching, the moment a wind passes the cloud, its shape scatters, it's foolish to think that's the cloud's strength, don't you think so, the opposite is also true, the cloud's strength didn't summon the wind, what decided that cloud isn't the shape of the cloud, the cloud I'm watching is the cloud that's lingered for five minutes, although for five minutes we might, slightly, have moved

YOUR FACE UNDER THE LIGHT

Past the road burning under the light, past the square with three people in it, past the hill of bees and honey, past the blue ash road, past the green train tracks, into the red river road, summer spring and winter pass, broken yellow-haired girls throw glass bottles out the window laughing, I, soaked through, burn under the light, and autumn passes, all the coins I owned disappear, your face spins under the light like merry-go-round horses clopping into your dreams

Under the streetlight the man playing trumpet shows off his black mole and laughs, sometimes you say you're happy, sometimes you say you're sad, your face under the light powdered so white you're unrecognizable, past the revolutionary road, past the only street, if you step on the bed's creaking footpath, my feet are the repeating last measure, a strange interlude playing slowly, theme forgotten

I, frozen in your fingers, unrecorded in your joints, passing through your eardrums, deflating like cold beer foam at the cheap pub where the jukebox's been running for thirty thousand years, your voices flow out only from your head, your voice can't pretend for one ten-thousandth of a second to be of this earth, transparent and beautiful pills bloom and scatter like flowers in the bottle of the man who drove away from the North Pole, the empty air where your raised fingers can't feel the deathly pitch or the silent knife edge

OLD BED

Hanging on my sides there might be fig seeds somebody spat out millions of years ago, fine strands of dust cover me like a hand-woven blanket, for a while now when I try to remember the breathing of the land above that's passed me by and the bright light shining down, my sides hurt

I'm not trying to say I've existed so long I can't remember the quiet noon, the work of keeping the body open in cracks of time, dead skin flakes landing from the sky open with long travel day and night, the ceiling grows remote

Blue dust, fine-grained fungus, my good soil, the leaves and stems of the figs inside me reach infinitely into phone lines, across the universe, and at some noontime, they will lightly stroke a prone woman's eyelashes. All the while I dream of that brilliant touch of the hand, all the while nobody visits me

MIDSUMMER SNOWBALL

Nobody swims
like fish
Just like airplanes don't fly
like birds
With me, without me
the summer sky is blue
and ice cream is sweet

The universe isn't round
like a snowball
You don't know
when you fell asleep
We become dark
then bright
Like it's just remembering, the window
shatters

MAYBE TOMORROW

Maybe tomorrow
there'll be old snow

Somebody's driving the car to the funeral home
You're not dead and I'm alive

Snow blows and blown snow
strikes the glass window and melts away

After landing in your black hair
and obliquely avoiding my black pupils

old snow leaves a stain on the window
and I erase the stain

Somebody throws a white flower
and we don't go back home

The song grows so faint we can't know the end
You're not dead and I'm alive

Maybe tomorrow
you and I and old snow

Part 2

A Strange and Bright Day

THE CHILDREN GROW

Just as a hat covers hair
and a white collar covers shoulders

the old are pregnant with the old
and children are pregnant with children

Where has the girl I loved gone?

From footsteps as small as a giraffe's
somebody else comes out running

When small footsteps cover each other
blood grows as warm as a river

CLOUD'S TABLE

Left side fourth shelf of the 25-Hour Supermarket,
a blue tin of sardines for 1400 won
Dust sits on it in a vortex
I pay 10,000 won and come back rattling two coins
Inside, seven deaths with bones in, or seven meals on the table

Sardines in front of the kitchen window, pointing sharp heads to the sky
Where have all the sardine heads gone?
Sudden rain and a cat sometimes prowl at the window
They leave their prints
But the rain is uninterested in the cat, the cat
in the rain, the rain in the sardines
I let their uninterested prints linger for days

A cloud sometimes gets invited
to my table, it quietly props its chin
and casts a shadow on me and my evening
Because it's hard to roll away a cloud
I drape the shadow to one side like a curtain and open the tin
Always seven sardine tins in front of my kitchen window
Seven types of death or seven types of luck

Past the three Tumbling games at New Generation Arcade
and the wide bench in front of Hyundai Real Estate
the 25-Hour Supermarket

I've never been there past midnight
I've only imagined the bright sign forgotten by the owner until morning
and on the left side fourth shelf of the 25-Hour Supermarket,
death pickled blue and an unmoving vortex
heaped for 1400 won each

CORRIDOR'S CHILD

At corridor's end
a child
While walking across the corridor
the child grows
with curly hair

With each echoing step
the child skips rope and grows
and gets rained on
From the window daylight and dark take turns
slapping the child's cheek

While walking across
the corridor the child grows taller
and blurred, smiles white,
hair grows down to cover feet,

windows open, close
In a child's throat making wind sounds
there's a black window
The wind blows right through

GRANDMOTHER'S BED

Benjamin begonia rubber tree leaves
When I watered the dead potted plant
its dream grew phrase by phrase
and climbed up clinging to my thin legs

I'll eat as little as a fish
and grow up into an adult who doesn't get periods
I'd known for ages
that my chick and puppy were eaten up
but Mom laughed like she was spilling a secret

I can't sleep
because of the night
because of the door handle
because of grandmother's bed
covered in a heavy sheet

My eyelids thin
During the day sunbeams stab my belly
Rubber tree coconut hibiscus
Are their roots
still buried under a jungle hot and humid
When I fill the fishbowl with water
the bubbles shooting up are like a question mark

My hair didn't grow pretty
because I ate around the beans
because I didn't pray
because of grandmother's bed
because the soil in the pot
dried up bright red

RADIO DAYS

The agency manager swore, *retarded son of a bitch,* one crazy hot summer
the dwarf man next door ate my dog and I hated his daughter's freckles,
I wanted to poke with a stick the swollen belly of Guk Hwa's mom who
was pregnant and smiling every season

I fell asleep imagining blue razor blades and red flowers, each morning
mom woke up in tears, *Aren't the blankets damp every night?* Freckles next
door showed her yellow teeth sneering, Sunday nights I wiped down
the silver bike, squatted next to the coal briquette ashes and peed, I
sweated a lot

We run away to a strange land, the fourth-dimension world where Nina
was trapped was always after school, before school and after school were
my only two worlds, the English teacher was an ugly woman, and I felt
there must be a long burn scar hidden under her blouse

It was freckles who showed me the red flowers, mom stopped waking
up in tears one morning, nobody sings songs anymore like *Stream water
where are you flowing flowing,* the silver wheel rolled away somewhere, and
I was the kid in the green steel gated house

SNOW WHITE

I wanted to learn the piano
White key black rod white key black rod
They were so shiny they made me sweat

When my black fingernails reflected on a shiny rod
I opened the teacher's powdered milk tin and ate on the sly
just two spoonfuls a day
but when the table was upset and the fish cut in half
      and she was snatched up by her hair
was that my fault?

On sunny days I play guitar on the rooftop
Just any song *pansies butterfly flowers cockscomb flowers*
If I fall off, the red rubber hose would stab my eyes

The cockscomb flowers open their lips *come here come here*
On singing days *butterfly flowers pansies cockscomb flowers*
Clouds and stairs and windows go round and round like Superman

I wanted to learn the piano truly
In the flower bed in the yard snails crawl around
On sunny days the insides of my ear are sticky

The sweaty guitar strings are rusting
Each day snails crawl about cut in half
On moonlit nights guitar on the rooftop
If I fall off the sharp stairs would stab my eyes

I DREAM OF SCHOOL

The pigeon house where machines sing with their black mouths
open, next to the tenderly pealing school gates
is my deskmate's head so we need to stick close to the walls

Walls where glass bottle shards glitter like press knives
A boy in work clothes shouts *Hey,*
Miss Pigeon, you dropped a feather

When space clouds come in screaming
it's time to hide in the air-raid shelter
While the airplane was crashing behind me
I touched his ear underneath the desk

I run,
I'm running,
the bridge has no guardrails,
a creek flows next to the guardrails
The calculation problems are eighth or sixteenth notes
And under the bridge the teachers eat a dog

When clouds come crowding in my head
that's when his eyes turn white with chalk dusk
The school is open like a privy hole late at night
like it's singing *Ah ah oh oh*

I AM A DARK-FACED CHILD

I am a dark-faced child
The season when flowers bloom in the yard
and tree bark smells tickle the nose
When auspicious things are happening

I am a dark-faced child
Relatives don't recognize me
Dust heaps on my head
Silver hair shining in the dark

I grow my hair and brush it nicely
I collect pebbles and dolls
Rose, cloud, sky
New wallpaper smelled strange

They came and went
and I without hunger
a dark-faced child
Dark hair white hair, even in dreams
you never recognized me

MY LOVE ELECTRICAL SUBSTATION

At night it feels like the whole city is crying, today twelve loggers came to the mountain and left, there are so many chimneys here clouds get caught in them sometimes, up in the mountain abandoned trenches split into branches

Do you like the park and the library there? Sometimes you sit on a bench eating lunch and watch the children on bikes, but the adults whistle, you've gone so far away and the only important thing here is the weather

The people here are sincerely scared of lightning, when you meet them on the street you can almost look right into their capillaries, we wear sweaters, the feeling of the atmosphere wandering about the city, do people still love there? When it rains I think about the things that can't help being rained on

At the end of the city there's an electricity generator and you used to walk all day to check it was there, the electric lines escape the sky endlessly, at night I raise the switch and buzz a little, does it rain over there and do clouds pass by and do people cry, are people scared of the lightning?

STELLA BEAUTY PARLOR

I'm a heavy woman, when I can't tell what I want I tidy my hangnails, I wanted to rise up, you come and go like a volatile afternoon washed away by golden dye, when number 1 you came out to meet me and waited I went into a motel room with number 2 you but while number 2 you slapped me because my knit undervest was embarrassing I shared mung bean pancakes with number 3 you and number 3 you vanished and number 4 you and I lived together a long long time but number 4 you grew taller and number 5 you left and I drank many cups of evaporating liquor and I telephone number 4 you, please draw the curtains, aren't there names like beauty parlor anymore? Every time I saw a mirror I mimicked your smile, not because I wanted to be younger, not because I wanted to be prettier, because I couldn't stand it, this is tricky, I didn't mean to become mysterious, it's just that something floated up, as meaningless as an ad blimp over a rooftop attic, that hair is not mine, I was always prosaic, am I growing as light as a joke?

MOVEMENT

Did you know her? I'm not talking about things like trembling or crying
but someone came in and out of her invisible circumference, the round
    pattern collapsed or made a different loop
If you could choose you could stay by her side or leave, one or the other,
    but did you know her?
It wasn't that she cried or laughed but she moved ever so slightly to the
    other side

SPRING SYMPHONY

I've buried three teeth in the flowerpot
Like pale green leaves piercing white seeds' flesh
I'm eight, twenty, twenty-seven

Grains of sand
in my brown eyes

The hospital ceiling was like a soaring UFO
The morning glory too were like crashed UFOs
I think it would be best
if my blood didn't pollute anyone

Is it true
that on a spring day with a wrinkled sheet flapping outside the window
if my voice gets a little louder and louder
I can sing songs I couldn't before?

Grains of sand under
my flowing blood

On a spring day when colorful notebooks
in the drawer say *me, me, me* and burn up
the tendrils are cut off with a hoe

A grain of sand
in my flapping shoulders

SYMBIOSIS

Those noiseless and impudent things started building a house, their lips grew fat and my hair ashen white, but what could I do? Around the time they dug in and settled in my cochlea, I often lost balance, my black eyes became windows, I absorbed all light well

It seemed my thick outer clothes became tatters and I was wearing newly woven clothes, like a thin glass window I shivered, all sounds could go through me, sometimes it seemed someone knocked wanting to ask a question, but I watched without giving off any smell, it seemed my eyes became very clear

Part 3
Hello, Goodbye

MY OWN LIFE

My eyes are my own
Making my eyes blink is my will
Turning around to look at you is also my will
My hand is my own
Smoking a cigarette
or rubbing it out is my will
Like smoke curling up and disappearing into air
my words come out of me
and flow into you
If you can't understand my words
that's not what I intended
Isn't that right?
One day you come to love someone
and the lights go on in the streets
then I go out into the streets
One day like the street lamps going off and on
you meet someone
and I'm pelted by pouring light in the street
But my will is still all mine,

CIRCUS

If I take off the hat
and raise the cane,
a white face and a short body.

The one and only time I confessed my love
the girl burst out laughing.
The ground moved further and further away
like I was on an air balloon
and silently I called for my mother.

It's hard to rest easy
if the elephants keep getting rashes.
I'll try whispering
Round mirrors are the best
as I braid my hair and wrap it around my head.

The rainbow ceiling I looked at above the net
is far away no matter where I am.
When the *Thorny Climbing Rose Rag* plays
let's heat up the dagger bright red in the fire.

Collecting the world map page by page
I write a letter
to fetch me.
The reverse of Friday is Sao Paolo.

Make a V and take a photo.
One teardrop dries fast
and the tights on the washing line dry fast too.
Like savannah cactus the weather's great.

SPIDER-MAN

The windows are lovely, clouds pass by, pigeons pass by, cold night and dirty placards flutter, buildings definitely aren't mazes, misunderstood beauty grows geometrically silent at night

The phone lines are tangled so I can't hear your voice, disappearing roads that disappear from behind and tangled roads, I can't figure out what I want on nighttime drives, meanwhile brilliant neon blurs eyes

You say you live faceless in a prison, from a faraway land he says *Hi* and I also say *Hi*, I asked *Is it bright over there*, he asked *How are you*

Under lights shining like insect eyes we threw the ball and caught the ball, in the dream ballpark we were impartial, I've never captured him, dirty clouds pass by geometrically, the windows shut neatly and dream, in silence, dazzled eyes

WE MEET

You were in there.

The moment the light shattered,
your arm crumbled

and a white ball flew out of you and far away

I turned my head with all my strength
and was blinded by the light.

You were in there and
It was quiet all around

but it seemed wet outside
as though it were raining from somewhere.

Green grass sprouted like lies
and you were running
in shoes red with mud.

SOUL OPENING EYES

Following the wrinkled road in your head
I walk heel to heel to the end

Like night bus windows
your pupils
reflect my filth

When music rings out
you'll probably get up and dance

It's okay if you open your eyes slowly
Oom pah pah oom pah pah

Did these two hands plant your hair?
A deep sandstorm blows into my throat

Mirages seeping out between my fingers
Marbles roll
and you'll probably move endlessly

Oom pah pah oom pah pah
There's no rest for us

BOOK OF BLOOD

You are a book of blood.
Your eyes' hot bundle of nerves connects all the way to your throat.
Thin pages fluttered from me.
Any incident can be contained in a book.
You record with your body.
My body's grains of sand,
the brilliant glass piercing my feet,
cold tomato flesh,
your blood is red, it fills you slowly
then cools.
Wind blew from somewhere just for a bit,
you can't read your present.
Because I don't want to promote anything
I've started speaking a foreign language
hoping one day it will be translated into blood.

YOU ARE MANET

You are Manet,
you are not decided
The air there is thin
You are not an object
You are a door
that is open or ambiguous
My eyes are sunken
and my ears can't hear everything
You are Manet,
you excite everything but
you begin from despair
You do not end
You are Manet,
but everything is freedom

SUMMER'S CALENDAR

There's me biting down on a green apple
and there's you who likes to split apples in four and peel them.

I watch clouds' ankles disappearing
while contemplating the clouds' changing shapes.
In the moment when ankle took away ankle,
your phone rings.

Summer clouds follow the atmosphere's rules.
Right foot first or left foot first,
they wanted to stand in front of the white line
when someone far away started running.

Your answering machine
contains only summer's voice.
And your calendar
begins on Mondays.

Clouds and green permeate the atmosphere
and disappear

and my summer calendar
begins on Sundays.

CHAIR

When you say *Ah* and open your mouth
lights of an overpass shot in burst mode
dimness of a sagging skyline
ashen feathers of a pigeon going home
shine, seep, flutter
A city rises from your mouth

I can find all kinds of things in you
When you say *Ah* and open your mouth
I enter a garden with many paths
Dinosaur-shaped shrubs
stoic broad leaves
tender and prim thorns
They aren't secrets
and I'm not an orphan there

I'm not an orphan there
We're facing each other on one chair
and another chair
You say *Ah* and open your mouth
and I can find all kinds of things in you
Yesterday, today, your
curtain rises

ON SATURDAYS WE LIKE THE NIGHT

Night seeps in
and you become dark

Your black pattern slashes across my eyes

You are a blond woman sitting vacantly on the bed
with a pleasant voice

Waves with unknown destinations
surge

I'm sure I've heard this song before
Sad four-eyes who's found out the show's secret

My mouth opens little by little

You're Saturday's wavering eyes
When bubbles scatter in the air
the song you were singing
comes out of my mouth

Blue waves float about the room
This song makes me feel good

MAIN ROAD

When the main road's sun rises over your right shoulder
and the sun draws a furrow over my left shoulder
I think about the vanishing point gathering at road's end with all its depth
and the indifference of the clouds above it.
Distant sunset, distant tree, distant house.
You talk about extinction but
the landscape trickles down like badly applied paint.
Sunset permeates
cloud,
tree,
house
But sunset is sunset and clouds are clouds
so airplane paths leave white marks in the sky.
When the main road's sun rises over your right shoulder
and the sun draws a furrow over my left shoulder
I observe without falling into thought
distant sunset, distant tree, distant house.
You talk about extinction but
I'll remember the five minutes of optical illusion
indifferent to you

OUR SUNDAYS

Since they say it'll snow tonight
let's boil a chicken and pick off its white flesh

Let's put on dresses
and go to the opera, on Friday nights
black-haired people from a cold country
sing *When I Met You*
sitting in a line on the second story

Saturday night newspapers
Sunday morning newspapers
They won't mention our names

Let's bury the puppy hit by a car in the flowerbed
and view the springtime
When pear blossoms fall, white clouds
tear through the netting and rise up
As we kiss
let's smash like glass fish the pupils of our eyes

Saturday envelopes
Sunday envelopes
They won't mention our names

DOORS

I can see a leaf of that door there being pushed by wind and one leaf of the door here opening, near and far vanished in a noiseless noon, it's hazy, the me reflected in the water glass wavers, briefly

Wrinkled layers of air prove you breathed in once a long time ago, it's a transparent reaction, I murmur *I only needed one gulp of air*

The sleep pooled in my body squirms, the water glass has been transparent for a long time, this is a cold hunger from long ago, who keeps eating away at my dream?

For a while I couldn't be seen often, I am a woman repeated in someone's nightmare, one leaf of that door there opened by the wind and a leaf of this door here closing, the water glass has been there for a while

SPRING DAY HELLO

You're in a little airplane

Milk cows sit and stand
Cars honk
Rosemary flutters in the wind

My eyes do whatever they want, goodbye,
hello, your propeller
has wrecked the tree in my backyard

You're not in the atmosphere
and I'm not on the ground
We all do whatever we want

Your muffler has scattered
my clouds

You on a spring day Hello

Part 4
Here the Nile, Here Kobe, Here Name Unknown

EARTHLY DINNER

We are surrounded by glass windows.
At night the lights go off and it snows.
The cutting boards are so clean.
Tangtangtangtang with strong wrists
I chop cabbage.
I set spoons and chopsticks
and soup and rice bowls.
The table is square and the ceiling round.
Three chairs, one in the corner.
The lights go on and it's your turn to sit.
Hrrrk, someone must be swallowing noodles.
Whose wrists are those julienning onions?
Tangtangtangtang a white and fierce smell.
A clear teardrop falls on the cutting board.
The windows bend round.
It's a bright indoor space
unclouded by steam.

FAR FAR NORTH

Looking down from a satellite, there's a city, and in the city there's the north side where you live. If you go up from there, there's your school perched precariously on a slope. The playground lying down quietly like a child and people crossing north to south on the river.

Looking down from a satellite to where you live, your house is like a box, and trees are as insignificant as matchsticks. You're like a dot, no, you can't be seen, and the line segment of a bird going into the distance is transparent. Maybe the bird was moving to the opposite side of your life.

The air is different here, this is my country. Like I'd just come back from a picnic far away, I wanted to talk about things not yet ended, but I can't tell where the beginning is. Here my body gets mixed in very easily, even though you're smiling right now.

Hello, I wave, hello, this is my country.

DREAM CATCHER

An island named Hidden Harbor. They say the dogs there watch the waves. And the rims of the dogs' eyes redden when the tail of the descending sky touches the beach.

While bad dreams hang dangling, I go on a walk. I laugh to myself because the flower-patterned water drops are pretty. If only I could live with the feeling of wearing skirts every day.

Was it the owner's fault he peeked into the dreams of the dog that got driven away? If you hang clusters of sausages from the ceiling and read Seton's wildlife books, winter comes quickly.

When the sun comes up, I'll sell ocarinas and dewdrop bracelets and rainbow hammocks. The night mends the valley's winds, hangs a day's labor on the net.

That's why no one could dream in place of the dogs. While waves come in forming water columns, we couldn't help but put our front paws meekly on the sand.

BEAUTIFUL DAYS

There's a place where golden light that looks like
it's crossed the Indian Ocean spills out
and blue steam flutters up
When a woman in a blinding white apron
scans the bar code noisily with those beautiful hands
my sleep runs away
I run away to a far far land
The volatile logo stamped on the crunching plastic bag
It's a beautiful day
A midnight store
open just for me

On rainy nights it's fine not to buy
crap like dry gin
Within the transparent glass doors it's chock full of
cold and colorful bottles and the music is
Goodbye, yellow brick road
Sometimes a yellow-dyed man pops out of storage
and the skinny folded umbrellas are ownerless
It's a beautiful day
When the doors close
it disappears into the frightening silence
Goodbye midnight store

MUSICS

It's snowing black
Click click
Slides slot in one by one in my retinas

I'm a ghost photographer
taking the same photo many times

Yet another roll of film unspools in your pupil

Your hair like cadenzas
one thread into many threads
many threads into many threads
split away from your cold skin

Every time your white eyelashes
click click close
snowflakes mix into your blood

Into the window frames
the black outside was slowly swelling

ECHO

Your ears
darkened the sofa you were sitting on.

Your eyes
darkened the TV you were watching.

Music you've never heard before
enters your body.

A face you've never imagined before
whirls out of you.

Fearfully multiplying elephants in search of water
go beyond the protected zone.

You shoot the elephant stepping on elephants that charges at you.
The elephants disappear into the light.

Your lights will be pressed flat.
They will be very thin and weightless.

THE EMPEROR OF BREAD

I saw the people's virtuous faces
When I sang with a rough and dirty voice
they threw me coins
Birds sang jingling in my chest

I want to scoop up the whitest flour
I want to make from seven kinds of grain
the most nutritious bread for them
I want to put sharp three-cornered hats on their families
and work them to death in the bread factory

Now the street musicians are singing
and I put on a suit and a medal
I am the emperor of bread,
they call me the god of bread

Humans only have one god
but I am the emperor of bread
I speak the language of only one country
and it's not what I eat
but they call me the god of bread

ELEVEN WINDOWS

The asphalt I can see from the eleventh floor
is cold and has an exact amount of road.

When it rains it rains so much,
even when raindrops touch the asphalt's heart
the cat sits motionless on the handrail.

From the eleventh floor the distance to the asphalt is wide
and eleven windows sit in order.
From between the eleven windows wind comes and goes
and white blankets flap and get folded.

The asphalt slowly heats
and each night turns cold.

The windows are open or closed
and a yellow light or white light turns on.
Children clatter like rats
but sometimes the light's off for a long time.

You live one floor below me
or a floor below that
or the very bottom floor.

I'm jealous of your garden
but I've decided to be content with the eleven windows
and the asphalt eleven floors below.

Friday slowly darkens.
My windows also turn cold.
On the weekend you visit yet another floor.

BEAUTIFUL BLUE DANUBE

Each night I eat some chocolate and ramen and fall asleep, it would be even better if there were some cold cola in the fridge but in any case I can't go back to the past, do you still come home at dawn like a wet cat?

I really love the German kitchen knife set I got for free from the butcher, when I hold the sleek black handles my heart races, but what are all these knives for, all I want to do is drink beer

A concerto really doesn't go with this night, *Beautiful Blue Danube*, cold water, your legs will be icy below the skirt, I haven't once dropped a knife handle

I'm fine, I can't go back, I snickered watching stand-up comedy and today I cooked for two whole hours, someday I hope to show you the brilliant *Made in Germany* label

Beautiful Blue Danube, just about now your black eyes should be shining in a freight train's last car, was it you who told me where the waters of the Danube start? You'll keep running and I'll munch on chocolate and peanuts, goodbye

BLACK AND WHITE MOVIE

If you visit there
you're a person from the past
You're soft and your clothes
are well arranged but
the skin I touched is no longer underneath
I'm scared
I weave my memories but
you don't have reason
I send you far away
and I fall asleep inside sleep
The sun spins endlessly
Your skin is so white
I can't look into my face
Even if you didn't go there
you come back
and you didn't come out of me

ABOVE THE HIGHWAY

We don't say hello
Let's meet in the middle tomorrow
Shading your eyes from lights stretching like gum
you smile crookedly
You run
past the cars the speed of light fluttering your hair
between the lights with their red heads up
You have no stage no chorus
You bend your back then straighten, you freely
spread your arms like a child on a balance beam
Wind scatters your scent
You only move when your pulse beats
We don't say goodbye
Looks like your ankles will be caught soon
by what doesn't go anywhere

MIDNIGHT TRAIN

This is a jungle,
yellow smoke rises
I cut you up night after night
You wait for me
Dreaming a long long dream
on such a filthy ship

On the midnight train
to the dreamland where you live

This is a marsh,
I have small eyes like a herbivore
Smelling your smell
I rise up
I arrive
While you drop me
into a deathlike sleep

On the midnight train
to the dreamland where you live

You're my stench
I'm going to bury you in a flowerbed
and water you with a little watering can every night

Your countless eyes
bloom like flowers
You're a place I've just left
A simpler and quieter place
than my world without you

On the midnight train
to the dreamland where you live

LIKE FLOWING RIVER WATER

When the coffee on the table evaporates
the long chair in front of the window on the veranda is lovely
Saturday classic films and 8 o'clock concertos and black goats
In the medicine packet, in the TV, in my pocket, in the freezer

Your two days
My three hours
Your Tuesday

Were my feet in the middle of turning white
in room 504
where the goose crawled into bed

Please remember that when I open the curtains
to both sides of my body, there are quite a lot of windows
and the dolphins floating on the Han River
Their exposed bellies must have been cold
The curtains disappear outside the lake
It's really nice that when you wake after sleeping you can sleep again

You left early Saturday morning
and must be racing on a signless highway
but maybe it isn't a highway
I really like my pathetic memory ability

RIDING A BIKE, I

Riding a bike, I
pass through salty sunlight and indifferent wind
Here the Nile, here Kobe, here name unknown

Does the surface of the land you walked on
wet the soles of your feet
When moisture brims up to your ankles
you put down roots
like a hollow plant
Roots stretching out from white ankles,
will you sprout leaves with the strength of your roots?
Time not slow not fast

Are you a little parched
or need some excitement?
Just like rain passes by beating you up
few things happen you can't tolerate
You simply walked
and arrived there
Time not slow not fast

Because your dreams are congested
your nights aren't a cradle
You keep turning people into passersby
and they keep watching the clouds pass above you

Some days are arid
but you don't intervene
Time not slow not fast

Rolling on my bike, I
mix shining drops of sweat in the dry wind,
here the Nile, here Kobe, here name unknown

ABOUT THE AUTHOR:

Ha Jaeyoun was born in 1975 in South Korea, and she received her bachelor's and doctorate degrees in Korean literature from Koryo University. In addition to Radio Days, originally published in 2006, she has published two other poetry collections in Korean as well as many scholarly works on modern and contemporary Korean poetry. Her work has also appeared in English translation in the collection Poems of Hwang Yuwon, Ha Jaeyoun, & Seo Dae-kyung.

ABOUT THE TRANSLATOR:

Sue Hyon Bae was born in South Korea and received an MFA in poetry at Arizona State University. She is cotranslator of the poetry collection A Drink of Red Mirror by Kim Hyesoon and has published a collection of original poetry in English, Truce Country.

ABOUT THE SERIES

The Moon Country Korean Poetry Series publishes new English translations of contemporary Korean poetry by both mid-career and up-and-coming poets who debuted after the IMF crisis. By introducing work which comes out of our shared milieu, this series not only aims to widen the field of contemporary Korean poetry available in English translation, but also to challenge orientalist, neo-colonial, and national literature discourses. Our hope is that readers will inhabit these books as bodies of experience rather than view them as objects of knowledge, that they will allow themselves to be altered by them, and emerge from the page with eyes that seem to see "a world that belongs to another star."